I BELIEVE

The Creed, Confession and the Ten Commandments

for Little Catholics

Neumann Press
Charlotte, North Carolina

I BELIEVE
The Creed, Confession and the Ten Commandments
for Little Catholics

CONTENTS

This edition copyright © 2013 Neumann Press. Neumann Press is an imprint of TAN Books.

These books, originally published under three separate covers, were first issued in 1953. This combined edition is published by Neumann Press.

ISBN: 978-1-930873-35-3

Printed and bound in the United States of America.

Neumann Press
Charlotte, North Carolina
www.NeumannPress.com
2013

THE TEN
COMMANDMENTS
for Little Catholics
Listen to God

BY SISTER M. JULIANA OF MARYKNOLL

ILLUSTRATED BY ADELE WERBER

Nihil obstat: John M. A. Fearns, S.T.D., *Censor Librorum*
Imprimatur: ✠Francis Cardinal Spellman, *Archbishop of New York*,
July 28, 1953

Neumann Press
Charlotte, North Carolina

GOD is wonderful and beautiful and very good. He made the world, with blue skies, trees, sunshine, grass and fruit. He made animals and birds. He made two people, Adam and Eve, to be the first father and mother of all the children in the world.

GOD is very wise. He knew what Adam and Eve must do to be good and happy. He told them, as plain as could be. All they had to do was listen to God, and mind what He said. But they did not mind God, so He made them leave their beautiful home. An angel with a sword of fire stood at the gate.

THEN the world became full of troubles. People began to fight and kill each other, and they lied and stole. They had to work hard for a living, and they got sick and died. After they died, they could not go to heaven, because heaven's door was shut. All these things happened because Adam and Eve did not listen to God.

AFTER a while, there were many people in the world, and nearly all of them were very bad. God thought, "I'm sorry I made them. I'll send a big flood and drown them all."

THERE was one good man, Noe, and his wife
and children. God told Noe, "Build yourself
a big boat, and go into it with your family." Noe
listened to God, and he and his big sons built
the boat. We call it the Ark. The bad people
made fun of Noe. "Building a big boat on dry
land! Ha! Ha!" they said.

WHEN the Ark
was finished, Noe
and his family went in-
side and they took a lot
of animals and birds
with them. Then God
shut the door and the
big rain began.

SOON the water was higher than the mountain tops. The bad people were drowned. Noe and his family were saved, because they had listened to God.

AFTER the big flood, the water dried up, and people began to live on the land again. There was a good man named Abraham who had a little son. The boy's name was Isaac. His father loved him more than anything else in the world.

ONE day God spoke to Abraham. He said,
"Take your little boy Isaac up on a mountain top. Tie his hands and feet and lay him on
a pile of wood. Then kill him and burn him up.
I want you to give him back to Me in this way."

ABRAHAM'S heart was breaking, but he knew he must mind God. He was just about to kill his son when God sent an angel to stop him. God didn't want Isaac to be killed. God wanted to see if Abraham loved Him more than Isaac.

ONCE there was a little baby named Moses. A bad king wanted to kill him, but his mother hid him in the weeds by the river. Moses grew up to be a good and holy man. One day, God called him to the top of a mountain and talked to him a long time.

GOD wanted everybody to know how to be good and happy. He wrote down ten rules on slabs of stone, and gave the stones to Moses. Moses read the rules to all the people. These rules are called the

Ten Commandments.

17

GOD is very anxious for us to be good and come to heaven with Him. So He also gave each one of us a little still voice inside. This still voice tells us when we have been good or bad. It is called our conscience.

BESIDES that inner voice, God gave us much more. He sent His only Son, Jesus, down from heaven to live in our world with us. Jesus showed us how to keep God's commandments. He even died on a cross to save us and open heaven. He taught us how to mind God.

THESE are the Ten Commandments God gave us to keep. In the first commandment, God says:

"I am your God. I want you to love Me more than anything else in the world."

We ought to think about God a lot. We should pray to Him often during the day, and especially at night and morning. We should be happy, because He loves us and takes care of us.

IN the second commandment, God says:
"My Name is holy and good. Be careful
to say My Name with love."

WE remember that God is listening, when we say His Name. We will be nice to all holy people and things, because they belong to God. If we hear anyone say God's Name in a bad way, we will whisper, "Blessed be God," to make up for it.

IN the third com-
mandment, God says:
"Sunday is My day.
Remember to keep
My day holy."

On Sundays and on
other holy days, we must
go to Mass. We should
also rest on those days,
and take time to think
more about God. We
might read a holy book
or look at holy pictures.
We should say more
prayers. We can also
play and be happy, be-
cause God loves us.

IN the ninth commandment, God says:
"You must not even think about nasty things."
God wants our hearts to be pure and holy. Then
we will be fit to live with God in heaven forever.

IN the fourth commandment, God says:
"Honor your father and your mother."

We must be nice to our fathers and mothers, if we want to please God. God has promised long life to children who are good to their parents.

I N the fifth commandment, God says:
"You must not hurt or fight
or be mean to people."

God is good to us. All the other people are His
children, too. We must be nice to them, because
God loves them.

IN the sixth commandment, God says:
"You must not do nasty things
that make you ashamed."
God knows what we think, and what we do,
and what we say. God is very holy, and we must
be holy in our bodies as well as in our souls.

IN the seventh commandment, God says:
"You must not steal."

We must not take money or other things from our parents or anybody else unless they give them to us. We should not keep things that other people have lost. We must not cheat.

IN the eighth commandment, God says:
"You must not tell lies about people."
God does not want us to say mean things about people, even if the mean things are true.

IN the ninth commandment, God says:
"You must not even think about nasty things."
God wants our hearts to be pure and holy. Then
we will be fit to live with God in heaven forever.

IN the tenth commandment, God says:
"You must not want other people's things."
God does not want us to be greedy and selfish.
He wants us to share our good things with others.

GOD our Father is very kind to us. He tells us how to get to heaven. All we need to do is to listen to God, and then mind His commandments. God always helps His children to be good. We shall love God, and love all His children in the whole world. Let us pray that everybody will listen to God, and keep His commandments.

I BELIEVE

A First Book on the Apostles' Creed for Little Catholics

BY SISTER M. JULIANA OF MARYKNOLL

ILLUSTRATED BY E. JOSEPH DREANY

Nihil obstat: John M. A. Fearns, S. T. D. Censor Librorum
Imprimatur: ✠ Francis Cardinal Spellman, Archbishop of New York, March 23, 1953

A CATECHETICAL GUILD BOOK

I believe in God.

GOD made me. He made me a person. He calls me by name. I am not like a dog or a cat. They cannot draw pictures. They cannot tell stories. They cannot think about God. But I can, because I am a person. I believe in God, even though I do not see Him. That is why God is so pleased to have me say, "I believe in you, dear God."

I believe in God.

I CANNOT see God, but I know Him, and I know that He loves me. He is everywhere, all around me. His ear is always close to my lips, so I can whisper little secrets to Him. If I am good, I shall see Him in heaven some day.

I believe in God the Father.

GOD wants us to know that He is our Father. He gives us everything we need. He takes care of us. He does not always give us everything we would

like, because He does not want us to grow up spoiled
and bad. He loves us too much for that. We should
love everybody because God loves us all.

I believe in God,
the Father Almighty.

God can do everything. He can give us brothers and sisters. He can take people away to heaven, when it is time for them to die. He holds the whole world in His hands. But there are some things God cannot do. He cannot be mean, or tell lies, or cheat.

*I believe in God, the Father Almighty,
Creator of Heaven.*

GOD made hundreds and thousands of strong, bright angels. He gave them a nice place called heaven to live in. Heaven is to be our home, too, if we are good and love God. The angels were good when God made them, but some of them turned bad. We call the bad ones devils.

41

*I believe in God, the Father Almighty,
Creator of heaven and earth.*

God made the beautiful world all for us. He made Adam to be the first father of all the people in the world. He made Eve to be Adam's wife. God said that, if Adam and Eve minded what He told them, they would never be sick or unhappy and they would never die. Some day they would go to heaven to be with God and the angels.

But Adam and Eve did not mind God. So heaven's door was shut. They could not get in. None of their children could get in, either.

I believe . . .
in Jesus Christ.

I believe . . .
in Jesus Christ, His only Son,
Our Lord.

AFTER Adam's sin, sickness and death came upon all people. Sadness and sin had made a great change. God did not want everyone to be lost like the bad angels. He thought, "I'll send my Son to save them." The name of God's son is Jesus Christ.

45

I believe . . .
in Jesus Christ, His only Son, Our Lord,
who was conceived by the Holy Ghost.

THERE is only one God, but there are three Persons in God. The three Persons are God the Father, God the Son, and God the Holy Ghost.

God the Son wanted to come from heaven and live with us. He wanted to open heaven, so we can live there and see God. He wanted to show us how good and kind God is. He wanted to teach us how to be good, so we will be a little like God.

47

I believe . . .
in Jesus Christ, His only Son, Our Lord,
who was conceived by the Holy Ghost,
born of the Virgin Mary.

AND God the Son became a little baby. His name was Jesus Christ. He was born in Bethlehem. The Holy Ghost gave Him the Virgin Mary to be His mother. Mary took care of Jesus until He grew up.

I believe . . .
in Jesus Christ, His only Son, Our Lord,
who was conceived by the Holy Ghost,
born of the Virgin Mary,
suffered under Pontius Pilate.

50

WHEN Jesus was a grown man, He went around doing good to everybody. He showed people how to love God and get to heaven. He cured the sick and even made dead people live again.

Some bad men hated Jesus. They wanted to kill Him. Pontius Pilate, the governor, wanted to please them. He said, "Jesus hasn't done anything wrong. Kill Him if you want to, but don't bother me."

I believe . . .
in Jesus Christ, His only Son, Our Lord,
who was conceived by the Holy Ghost,
born of the Virgin Mary,
suffered under Pontius Pilate,
was crucified, died.

THE bad men nailed Jesus to a cross and let Him die. Jesus wanted to die, because that was the way He opened heaven for us. He loved us, and He loved everybody in the whole world. He wanted everybody to live in heaven with Him forever.

I believe . . .
in Jesus Christ, His only Son, Our Lord,
who was conceived by the Holy Ghost,
born of the Virgin Mary,
suffered under Pontius Pilate,
was crucified, died and was buried.

MARY, the mother of Jesus, stood by the cross and cried. The bad men would not let her help Him. When Jesus was dead, some good men helped take Him down from the cross. They went with Mary and laid His dead body in a cave. They put a big rock in front of the door to the cave and went home. They were very sad.

He descended into hell.

HEAVEN had been shut ever since Adam and Eve had sinned. Many good people had died, but they could not get into heaven. They had been waiting a long time, in a special place which is called hell, although it is not the same hell where the devils live. As soon as Jesus died, His soul went down and told all the good people that He had made up for Adam's sin. Soon they would go to heaven with Him. How happy they were!

I believe . . .
the third day He rose again
from the dead.

THREE days after Jesus died, He came back to life. He visited His Mother Mary and all His friends. How happy they were!

I believe . . .
He ascended into heaven.

JESUS stayed with His friends a while. He told them all about the holy Church He was going to start. He told them to go out and tell everybody in the world about Him. He wanted everybody to belong to His Church. When Jesus had finished teaching His friends, He went up to heaven.

I believe . . .
He ascended into heaven,
sitteth at the right hand of God,
the Father Almighty.

In heaven, Jesus sits beside God, His Father. He waits for us to come and live with Him in heaven. He has built beautiful houses there for us to live in.

I believe . . .
from thence He shall come to judge
the living and the dead.

Some day Jesus will come again and all men shall see Him in the sky. The dead will come to life again. We all will stand before Jesus. His clear bright eyes always see whether we have been good or bad. He will take the good people into heaven to live with God and the angels. The bad people will have to go to hell.

I believe in the Holy Ghost.

God the Father made the world and all of us. God the Son became Man and died on the cross to save us. God the Holy Ghost came to us when we were baptized. He makes our souls holy. He is also called the Holy Spirit. Spirit means breath or wind. We cannot see the wind but we know when it is blowing. We cannot see the Holy Ghost. Sometimes we draw His picture as a white bird. But the Holy Spirit is not a bird. He is God. The Holy Ghost lives in us when we are good.

60

believe in . . .
the Holy Catholic Church.

JESUS started His Church to help us be good. The Holy Ghost takes care of the Church and makes it holy. Jesus stays with His Church all the time, because He loves us and wants to be near us. At Holy Mass Jesus gives Himself again to His Father, just as He did on the cross, to keep heaven open and make up for our sins. At Holy Communion He comes to visit us.

I believe in . . .
the communion of Saints.

SOME people who die are good, but not quite good enough to go to heaven right away. They go to a place called purgatory where they wait until their souls are worthy to enter heaven. We can pray for these people; they can pray for us. Besides this, the saints in heaven pray for us all. All the people of God's Church are like a great body. With Jesus as our head, we make up what is called "The Mystical Body of Christ."

I believe in . . .
the forgiveness of sins.

JESUS made up for all our sins when He died on the cross. He wanted our souls to be beautiful and clean. And He made it easy for us to keep them clean. Jesus gave His priests the power to wash our souls clean and white. But we must be sorry for our sins and promise not to disappoint Jesus again. At confession, we can think we see Jesus sitting there in the priest's place.

*I believe in . . .
the resurrection of the body
and life everlasting.*

EVERYBODY must die some day. Jesus died because He wanted to make up for the sin of Adam and for our sins. Jesus came back to life again, to show us that we, too, will come back to life. When He comes to us in Holy Communion it

is a promise that we, too, will live forever. We will be bright and beautiful, like Jesus. We will never again be sad or sick or hurt, and we will never die any more. We will be with God and the angels in heaven forever.

This prayer is called the Apostles' Creed. The Apostles were the friends of Jesus. They wanted us all to know just what Jesus taught them, so they made up the Apostles' Creed and wrote it down for us.

THE APOSTLES' CREED

I BELIEVE *in God the Father Almighty, Creator of heaven and earth; and in Jesus Christ, His only Son, Our Lord; who was conceived by the Holy Ghost, born of the Virgin Mary, suffered under Pontius Pilate, was crucified, died, and was buried. He descended into hell; the third day He arose again from the dead; He ascended into heaven, sitteth at the right hand of God, the Father Almighty; from thence He shall come to judge the living and the dead. I believe in the Holy Ghost, the Holy Catholic Church, the communion of saints, the forgiveness of sins, the resurrection of the body and life everlasting. Amen.*

MY CONFESSION

For Little Catholics

BY

FRANCIS McGRADE

PICTURES BY

MIMI KORACH

W E MUST always do what God wants us to do. He gave us our parents to guide us. If we do something that does not please our parents they are offended.

When we are sorry for doing wrong, and tell our parents so, they forgive us.

We show that we are really sorry by trying to make up for the harm we have caused.

Anything we do that displeases God is called a sin. We must be sorry for every sin and tell God we are sorry for our sins and ask Him to forgive us. If we are really sorry, He forgives us, as our parents do. He has given us the Sacrament of Penance to let us be forgiven. When we go to confession we are receiving this Sacrament of Penance.

In confession we tell our sins to a priest, who is sent by Jesus. Jesus really hears our sins and forgives us through the priest.

Through Baptism our souls are made pure and beautiful as flowers with the life of God.

But when we commit sin our soul begins to lose its beauty. The divine life fades like the flower, even though the sin is little and called venial.

A big sin is called mortal, because it takes away God's life of grace. The soul dies like the dead flower.

The Sacrament of Penance gives the life of God back to the soul.

These are the five things we all have to do when we go to confession. Be sure to remember them. We will talk about them one at a time.

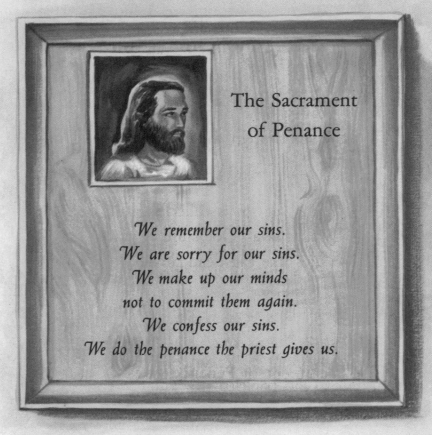

The Sacrament
of Penance

We remember our sins.
We are sorry for our sins.
We make up our minds
not to commit them again.
We confess our sins.
We do the penance the priest gives us.

We Remember Our Sins

First we have to remember the sins we have committed. We should pray to the Holy Ghost to help us remember our sins.

Here are some sins we may have committed:

Did I miss Mass on Sunday through my own fault?

Did I come late?

Did I misbehave in church?

Did I think of other things when I should have been praying?

Did I use the name of God without showing reverence to God?

Did I eat meat on Friday when I knew it was Friday?
Did I disobey my parents or my teachers?
Was I stubborn or mean to them?
Did I make fun of them?
Did I talk back to them?

Did I quarrel with anyone or fight?
Did I hate anyone?
Did I do anything mean to anyone or wish him harm?
Did I say mean things about anyone or listen to them?
Did I do anything impure?

Did I steal anything or keep anything that wasn't mine?

Was I careless with other people's property?

Did I tell lies?

Is there anything else bad I did at home? At school? At church? When I was playing?

We Are Sorry for Our Sins

When we do something that displeases our mother, she will forgive us if we are truly sorry. If we are not sorry, we do not deserve to have mother forgive us.

If we are really sorry for our sins, God will forgive us—but He will not forgive us if we are not sorry in our heart.

We should be sorry for our sins, most of all because they offend God. He loves us. No persons with mortal sins on their souls can go to heaven when they die.

We should be sorry for each and every sin.
Sin is the only thing in the world that is really
bad. We must be free from all of our sins before
we can see God.

We Make up Our Minds Not to Commit Them Again

If we are really sorry for displeasing God, we will promise Him not to do wrong again.

When we are really sorry for sin, we should make up for the harm we have done. We must give back anything we have stolen. If we have broken anything we must fix it or replace it.

We Confess Our Sins

After we have prepared ourselves well, we are ready to make our confession. We take our place in line. When our turn comes, we walk into the confessional and kneel down.

When the priest opens the slide so he can hear us, we say:

"Bless me, Father. I confess to Almighty God and to you, Father, that I have sinned."

Next we tell the priest how long it has been since our last confession. If we cannot remember exactly, we tell as nearly as we can remember. If this is our first confession, we tell him so.

Then we tell the priest our sins. One must tell him all the mortal sins committed since the last confession, if one has been to confession before. We should also tell our venial sins to have them forgiven.

1. I am the Lord thy God, thou shalt not have strange gods before Me.
2. Thou shalt not take the name of the Lord thy God in vain.
3. Remember thou keep holy the sabbath day.
4. Honor thy father and thy mother.
5. Thou shalt not kill.
6. Thou shalt not commit adultery.
7. Thou shalt not steal.
8. Thou shalt not bear false witness against thy neighbor.
9. Thou shalt not covet thy neighbor's wife.
10. Thou shalt not covet thy neighbor's goods.

When we have finished confessing our sins, we say:

"I am sorry for these, and for all the sins of my past life, especially for.................................."

(Here we add some sin for which we have been very sorry in the past. God is pleased when we keep our hearts sorry for all the sins of our life.)

Anyone who commits a mortal sin must tell how many times it happened. Sometimes people cannot remember the exact number. Then they must try to come as close as they can. We should also try to remember how many times we committed each venial sin.

Now the priest talks to us. This is like having Jesus Himself talk to us. The priest is speaking for God, to help us become better.

The priest gives us our penance. We must listen carefully so we shall remember what to do when we leave the confessional.

These are prayers that are often given as penances:

THE OUR FATHER

Our Father, who art in heaven, hallowed be Thy name; Thy kingdom come; Thy will be done on earth as it is in heaven. Give us this day our daily bread; and forgive us our trespasses as we forgive those who trespass against us; and lead us not into temptation, but deliver us from evil. Amen.

THE HAIL MARY

Hail Mary, full of grace! The Lord is with thee; blessed art thou among women, and blessed is the fruit of thy womb, Jesus. Holy Mary, Mother of God, pray for us sinners, now and at the hour of our death. Amen.

The priest tells us to say an Act of Contrition. We should say it softly and mean every word. We must be sorry from the bottom of our heart.

Act of Contrition

O my God, I am heartily sorry for having offended Thee, and I detest all my sins, because of Thy just punishments, but most of all because they offend Thee, my God, Who art all-good and deserving of all my love. I firmly resolve, with the help of Thy grace, to sin no more and to avoid the near occasions of sin.

Finally, the priest gives us absolution when he speaks these words: I absolve thee from thy sins in the name of the Father, and of the Son, and of the Holy Ghost. Amen.

We leave the confessional when the priest closes the slide. A great joy often comes over us then. Sanctifying grace which Christ gained for us by His death has poured into our soul. If a soul was sick with sin, it now shares again in the life of God.

We Do the Penance the Priest Gives Us

Now we thank God for taking our sins away, and we also pray for the priest. But most important, we do the penance the priest gave us. The Sacrament of Penance always takes away the punishment of hell. But this other penance which the priest gives in the confessional helps to take away all other punishment.

When our soul is in the state of grace, we share the life of God Himself! This means that God makes us worthy to live with Him forever. Then we are more than just children of earth. Grace makes us true children of Our Father in heaven, Who now wants us to receive His son Jesus as our food in Holy Communion.